TopReaders

Coral Reefs

Robert Coupe

Contents

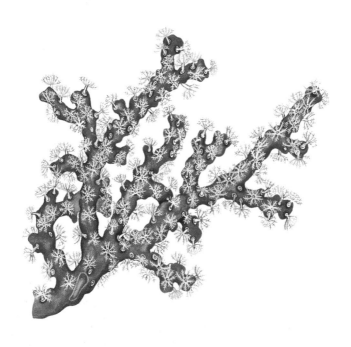

A coral reef is built from the skeletons
of tiny sea animals. It takes thousands
of years to grow. Coral reefs exist
in shallow seas in warm parts of the world.
Corals have many shapes and colors,
and many sea creatures live among them.

What Are Corals?

Corals are very unusual sea animals.
They have soft bodies, and they build
hard skeletons around these bodies.
As they grow, corals leave these skeletons
behind. The skeletons build up the reef.

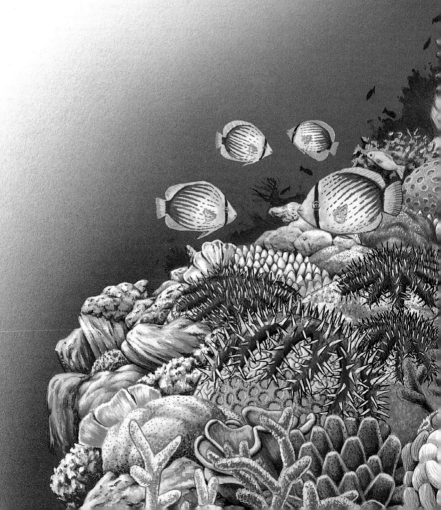

Coral reefs provide food and shelter for many kinds of sea plants, fish, sponges , shellfish , and some sharks.

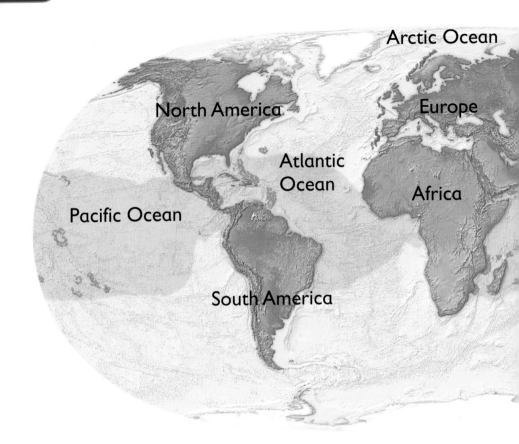

North America

Arctic Ocean

Europe

Atlantic
Ocean

Africa

Pacific Ocean

South America

Where Are They?

This map shows where coral reefs exist.
Most corals grow in warm seas and oceans.
A few reefs are in colder, deeper waters.
More than one-third of all coral reefs
are in seas near Australia and Indonesia.

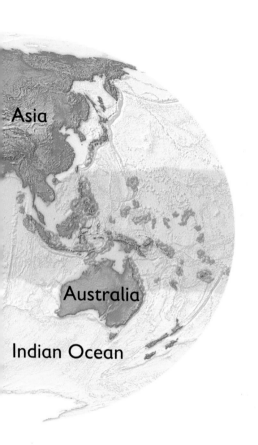

Asia

Australia

Indian Ocean

Fact File

As a coral reef grows older, more sea animals come to live on it. Some of the oldest reefs are in warm parts of the Pacific and Indian oceans. Reefs in the Atlantic are younger.

Key

■ warm water corals
🔸 cold water corals

Most corals are only about as big as a grain of rice. They grow a hard skeleton and have many arms, called tentacles . These have a sting in them.

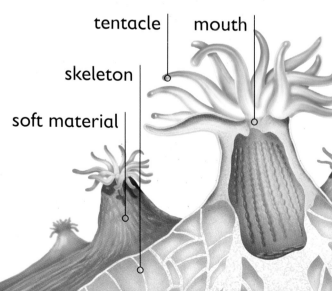

tentacle   mouth

skeleton

soft material

Atolls

An atoll is a coral reef that surrounds
a body of water, or lagoon . Often,
an atoll also has some land or sand in it.
Palm trees or other plants may grow there.
Atolls begin as volcanoes in the sea.

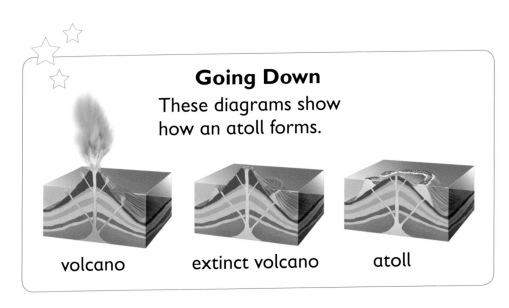

Going Down
These diagrams show
how an atoll forms.

volcano   extinct volcano   atoll

A volcano that rises out of the sea can slowly wear away
until it is just a small island with a coral reef around it.
The island, too, wears away and sinks under the water.

reef

trees and plants

sand and soil

Parts of an Atoll

As a volcano sinks slowly under the sea,
coral grows upward on its sides.
When the coral reaches the surface
of the water, it dies. Soil can form
on top of it. Some plants may grow.

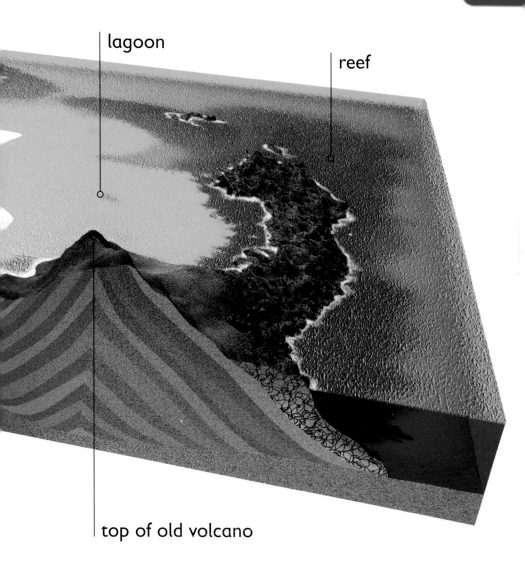

lagoon

reef

top of old volcano

The soil that forms on a coral atoll comes from seeds dropped by birds and from soil that the sea washes in. This soil is not deep. Only plants with shallow roots can grow in the soil on these atolls.

Great Barrier Reef

Coral reefs can grow to be very large. The Great Barrier Reef is near the coast of eastern Australia. It is the longest reef of all. It is 1,250 miles (2,000 km) long and, in some parts, 95 miles (150 km) wide.

Many Fish

More than 2,000 types of fish live on the Great Barrier Reef.

harlequin tuskfish

Corals have built up the Great Barrier Reef over millions of years. It now contains about 3,000 separate coral reefs. Around 350 different types of coral live there.

Colorful Corals

All living things are made up of cells . Sunlight acts on plant cells that live inside corals to produce their colors. Corals come in all colors, sizes, and shapes. Reefs often look like undersea gardens.

dead man's fingers

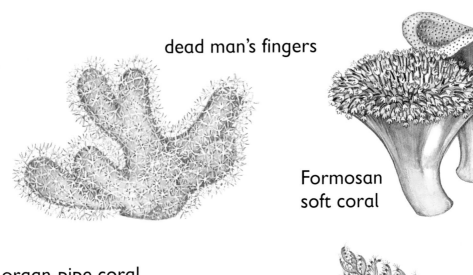

Formosan soft coral

organ-pipe coral

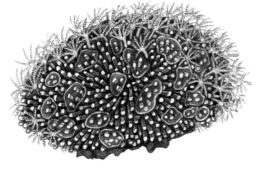

sea pen

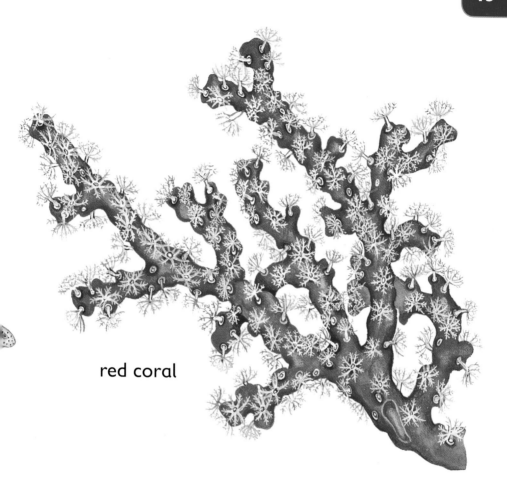

red coral

Corals grow into many different shapes. Some of these shapes remind us of other things. That is why we name some kinds of corals after things that we think they look like.

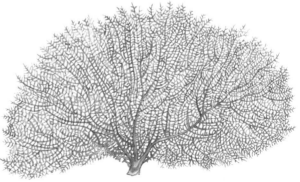

West Indian sea fan

Brain Coral

Brain coral lives in warm, shallow waters. It is called a stony coral because it is hard on the outside. It has ridges all over it. Coral animals live in the grooves that run like little valleys between these ridges.

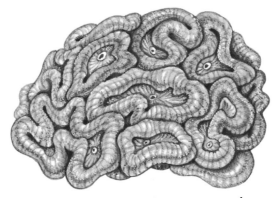

red brain coral

Brain coral gets its name because its shape looks like the shape of a human brain. This coral can live for 200 years. Masses of brain coral sometimes grow 6 feet (1.8 m) high.

Fact File

Brain coral is strong.
Its hard surface and rounded
shape help protect it from
storms and tides.

Bubble Corals

Bubble corals may look like creamy grapes. But they have tentacles that can sting other corals nearby. During the day, the bubbles are filled with water. At night, they go down when the water empties out.

Tentacles

The tentacles of some soft corals look a lot like feathery flowers.

Bubble corals live in large groups. Each of the bubbles is a separate coral animal. They grow on reefs in shallow seas between the continents of Africa and Australia.

Hiding

Many animals can be very hard to see.
They match the colors and shapes
around them. Coral provides good
hiding places. Many animals
blend with it.

A lot of fish and other sea creatures
have colors and shapes that hide them.
We say that these creatures have
camouflage . Brightly colored fish
often swim unseen among
colorful corals.

Coral Fish

Lots of different fish live on coral reefs.
Many are as colorful as the corals
around them. Some have bright patterns.
That is why we call them names such as
butterflyfish, parrotfish, and clownfish.

splendid toadfish

*Coral trout can be red, brown, or dark green. They have
bright blue spots. Their color can change at different times
of the day, or when they move to new parts of the reef.*

Reef Hunters

A coral reef looks like a peaceful garden, but there are hunters lurking there. Sharks attack fish. Larger fish feed on smaller ones. Octopuses catch crabs and jellyfish sting their prey.

The gray reef shark is just one of several sharks that hunt on reefs. Different sharks catch different fish, so they do not compete for food.

clownfish

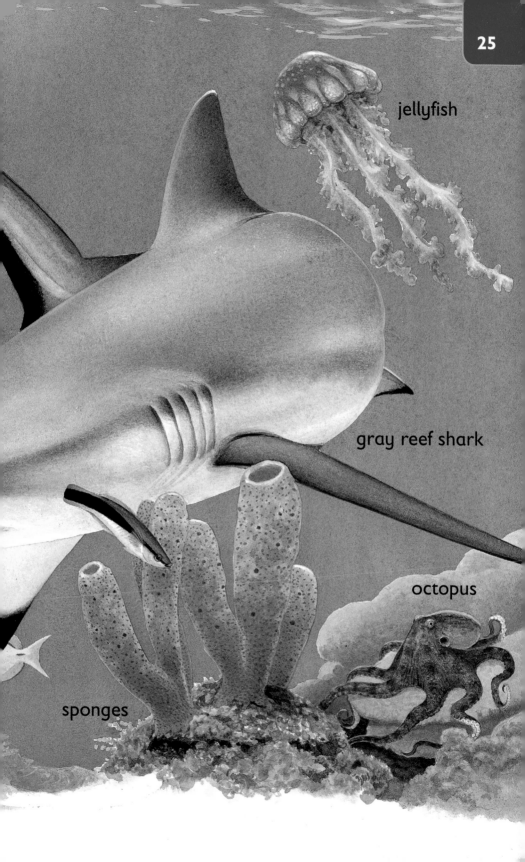

jellyfish

gray reef shark

octopus

sponges

Cleaners

Tiny animals live on the bodies of some fish and sharks. We call them parasites . Some shrimps eat parasites on fish. A colorful shrimp that cleans fish is the coral banded shrimp.

Good and Bad

Coral banded shrimps do a useful job. Crown of thorns starfish feed on coral and damage the reef.

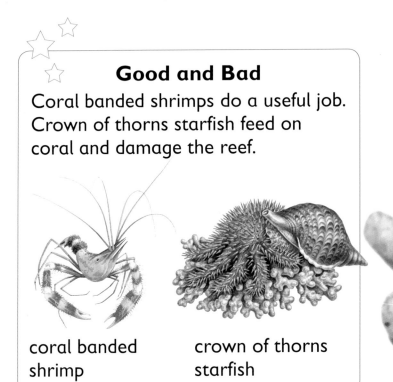

coral banded shrimp

crown of thorns starfish

Cleaner shrimps live on coral reefs. They often work in groups as they clean parasites from fish. They even go into the mouths of some fish.

Reefs and People

People enjoy coral reefs for their beauty. But some of the things humans do can damage reefs. Soil from farms can smother coral. Substances, such as oil, in the water are also very harmful.

rubbish left on a reef

Many scientists now study coral reefs and the creatures that live among them. Using modern diving gear, they can observe corals and fish at very close quarters.

Quiz

Can you unscramble the words and match them with the right pictures?

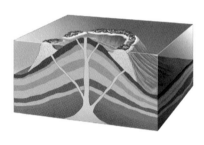

LATLO

DRE ORCAL

MSPIRH

STUFSHIK

Glossary

atoll: one or more coral reefs that surround a lagoon

camouflage: the color or shape of an animal's body that makes it hard to see in its surroundings

cells: the smallest parts of any living plant or animal. Many animals' bodies consist of billions of cells.

cleaner shrimps: shrimps that eat animals that live on the bodies of fish

coral reef: a mass of rocky material in parts of the ocean, made up of the skeletons of tiny sea animals called corals

lagoon: a kind of lake in the sea. Water in a lagoon is surrounded by sand, rocks, or coral reefs.

parasites: animals or plants that get their food by living on another animal or plant

ridges: long, narrow ranges of hills or mountains on land or under the sea

shellfish: a water-living animal that has a body covered with a shell. Crabs, lobsters, and shrimps are shellfish.

skeletons: all the bones in animals' bodies

sponges: sea animals with soft bodies that can hold water easily. Sponges live together in very large numbers.

tentacles: long, thin, wavy parts outside some animals' bodies. Some animals have poison in their tentacles.

volcanoes: mountains that can explode, spurting hot ash, gases, and melted rock from under Earth's surface

Index